Helena Christensen in 100% Fair Trade
& Organic Cotton dress designed by
Bora Aksu for People Tree, shot
by herself for Japanese Vogue.

At People Tree we always knew we had a unique story. It's been told by Vogue, modelled by Helena Christensen and Lily Cole and won us lots of ethical and business awards.

But we wanted a retail fashion giant to listen to our story, and we were thrilled when *asos.com* did. The innovative online store is now offering a People Tree range for its customers and is helping us to spread a conscious fashion message further afield.

Every extra pound you spend helps the people who make garments for People Tree. And it means much more than that. Every single purchase demonstrates to the fashion industry that there is demand for Fair Trade fashion, and on that they will base their decisions about how they buy clothing in the future. Thank you, *asos.com*, for that opportunity.

This book explains why you should buy Fair Trade.

## People Tree

Made possible by generous support of:

# Fair Trade Fashion:
## an agenda for change.

Welcome to *By Hand*. This book sets out the story behind Fair Trade Fashion. It is a celebration of the hand skills and artistry of those who make and design for People Tree. *By Hand* offers a new model for fashion, showing how investing in communities and their environment creates a blueprint for sustainable fashion.

Fair Trade can help people help themselves to better nutrition, health, education, and community development, and protect their environment. The Fair Trade fashion industry puts food on the tables of the poorest families, enables parents to send their children to school and to escape a vicious cycle of poverty described to you in the interviews that follow. This book demonstrates that fashion that is Fair Trade, natural and handmade is not only beautiful, it is vital to our planet and its people.

## A fashion history less heard

At the height of British colonial power in 1850, India, Bangladesh and Pakistan were one country. The British Empire systematically undermined local Indian textile cottage industries that had produced cloth and clothing by hand for millennia, destroying countless livelihoods so they could sell British mill-made fabrics to the subcontinent. In years to come, Gandhi identified how this kind of forced trading eroded India's traditional livelihoods, sense of community and peace.

The muslin weavers of Dhaka, the capital of Bangladesh today, were famous throughout the world for their dexterity. To this day, people speak of handwoven cloth so fine that a whole sari could pass through a wedding ring. The mill-made fabrics from the British could not begin to compete. After trying to prohibit handweaving, the British cut off the middle fingers of master weavers. The skill was lost.

## Man over machine

Today, synthetic fibres, yarns and machine-made fabrics have largely replaced handmade, natural and biodegradable fabrics and clothing. Nevertheless, in India handweaving is still the second biggest industry after agriculture and continues to provide an income for millions of families. A handloom costs less than £100, and even the poorest household can earn a living.

Crafts and cottage industries receive little acknowledgement, but feed countless households. Hand embroidery, block printing, natural dyeing and organic cotton farming all provide valuable work in the most rural areas of the developing world. Handskills enrich communities economically, socially and culturally. As the world population grows, people's hands have become our most plentiful natural resource. We are running out of oil, exhausting water supplies and dangerously overburdening the planet with toxic chemicals. Hand production and traditional farming hold the key to reducing $CO_2$ emissions.

*By Hand* shows how the indigenous skills of Asia, Africa and Latin America can bring social and environmental justice together. Fair Trade projects deserve your support in promoting fashion that respects people and the planet.

*Fair Trade doesn't just mean paying a fair price. It is an entirely different way of doing business, where the objective is not profit at any cost, but to help people in the world's most marginalised communities escape poverty and protect the environment. People Tree actively supports 50 Fair Trade producer groups in 15 developing countries and collaborates with designers to bring exclusive Fair Trade and sustainable fashion to the catwalk.*

# ABOUT THIS

# BOOK

This book is the story of People Tree, in our own words.
I started the story in 1991 in Japan, and 14 years later found myself
sitting at the World Economic Forum in Davos (see my diary,
right).

I have recorded and photographed the artisans
and suppliers of the People Tree clothing and jewellery collections,
and spoken to our designers and mentors. Special thanks to Miki
Alcalde, who helped with the book photography.

And our fashion photographers have chronicled
the love and artistry that goes into garments that are Hand Made.

Safia Minney
*Founder of People Tree*

# MAKING ECONOMICS

# MAKE SENSE

*People Tree at the World Economic Forum in Davos, 2008*

The World Economic Forum 2008 has brought together 2,300 business leaders, experts from leading development agencies and NGOs, foundations, universities and think-tanks – and 40 of us 'social entrepreneurs'. That is, people like me who use a 'business model', running different companies and organisations at grassroots level, creating livelihoods for the most marginalised people, protecting their rights and the environment. So many influential people together in one place to debate and find solutions to the world's problems – so how quickly can we change course, and what are we up against?

I've always thought that someone should write a pocket guide to economics explaining in simple language how the so-called 'free' market system is not free at all. I'm sure that's why I gave up my economics A-level half way through. The 18th century economist Adam Smith, in his book 'Wealth of Nations', developed the idea that, through trading freely between lots of buyers and sellers, all knowing anything they need to know, society would allocate use of resources automatically in the most productive way for the benefit of society as a whole (he called this the workings of an 'invisible hand'). This theory has been wildly popular ever since. People love the idea that things can work out for the best because of, not despite, the inherent greed of people involved.

Prices rarely include the real social and environmental cost. As businesses 'helpfully' advise governments, we often get subsidies, trade restrictions and regulations which keep smaller producers out of the market. Adam Smith warned against all these things, but not in my textbooks. It doesn't take a very bright 17-year-old to recognise that so-called 'free markets' aren't free markets at all – the invisible hand is in invisible handcuffs, and cannot do its work. Presumably most of the business elite at Davos can see this too, but for some reason the debate always starts on the premise that we have to have a 'free' market, and anything extra on top that the business community does for society is really sweet of them to do.

A pocket guide to economics that tells it like it is could save a lot of time at events like the World Economic Forum. It might cut down some of the 220 or so meetings over the 5 days in Davos. More importantly, it would also help to foster honest dialogue, perhaps slow down the exploitation of the world's natural resources, maybe even help over a billion people to escape the poverty trap. Furthermore, it could help to nurture a better kind of economics and business graduate, future business leaders and policy-makers.

In one workshop on Corporate Social Responsibility, a leading union representative reminded participants that International Labour Organisation (ILO) labour standards have been agreed by all nations some fifty years ago, so it shouldn't take formal meetings of the great and good to start talking about actually meeting them. In practice, the prices of products we buy do not reflect the living costs and meeting basic human rights of the people making them. If companies were simply to meet their legal obligations on labour rights and environmental regulations, poverty and pollution would be reduced on a massive scale. Yes, products might cost a bit more, but personally, I'd rather pay a bit more now, than pay later in the form of runaway climate change and the global unrest millions of environmental refugees on the move will bring. All developed nations got to where they are today by protecting their own markets and people until they reached a certain level, so not allowing developing nations to do the same is obviously hypocritical. The theory of markets that underpins economic ideology only works as a theory if it can assume 'perfect information' – information available to both buyer and seller. Putting the information back into the market is what Fair Trade does. Acting in long term partnership with the producers to help them understand the market, and getting the information about the real social and environmental cost to the consumer, in an increasingly complicated world.

I am sure Adam Smith would have been a great fan of Fair Trade. Just as when Gandhi imagined the uncontrollable monster that globalisation would become in depriving people of their basic human rights, Smith would have seen Fair Trade as a Global Village, a movement of people supporting each other, building an alternative economy first, creating critical mass, and then campaigning to make it the norm.

That is why, at the same time as People Tree is supporting groups of people in the developing world – artisans, farmers – we are campaigning for change internationally. We know that policy agreed in five-star conference venues is liable to miss the needs of the poor. The Fair Trade, environmental and social enterprise movements have lots of good ideas that are tried and tested, and many have received worldwide acclaim.

Now is the time to scale these up.

# ORGANIC COTTON

Fair Trade Organic Cotton less than 1%

→ Cotton bought in the UK

**Fair Trade cotton accounts for less than 1% of the total amount of cotton sold in the UK.**

→ The Moral Fibre

The conventional cotton industry has a devastating effect on farmers and the environment. Heavy pesticide use reduces biodiversity, disrupts ecosystems, and contaminates water supplies. Worse still, pests exposed to synthetic pesticides build up a resistance to them so each year, farmers have to buy and use more pesticides to grow the same amount of cotton. Not only does this increase the annual damage to the environment, it means the farmer gets less and less profit from the crop. Many chemicals used in cotton farming are acutely toxic. At least three of them are in the 'dirty dozen' – so dangerous that 120 countries agreed at a UNEP conference in 2001 to ban them. So far this hasn't happened. If we pay farmers a higher price for their cotton, they can diversify their crops, use less polluting farming methods and protect the environment.

Conventional Cotton more than 99%

→ 2.5% of all farmland worldwide is used to grow cotton

→ 10% of all chemical pesticides are sprayed on cotton.

→ 22% of all insecticides are sprayed on cotton.

Photography: Andreas Pohancenik + Ting Lu   Model: Matt Pascoe

→ The World Health Organisation estimates
20,000 farmers die a year as a result
of the use of agricultural pesticides in
developing countries.

# WATER ISSUES

→ **Cotton and pesticides**

Pesticides and insecticides not only undermine farmers' health, production of agro chemicals consumes a lot of oil and releases a great deal of $CO_2$. With oil supplies set to peak in 2012 and starting to fall off, we have to find alternatives to oil-intensive farming methods now. Buying organic and natural-based farming can give farmers the opportunity to change now, before it's too late. Organic and Fair Trade cotton has helped to reduce water consumption by over 60% in Gujarat, by helping farmers invest in drip irrigation. As water scarcity becomes as big an issue as global warming, this is critical.

→ **It takes over 2,000 litres of water to produce the average t-shirt.**

→ **Organic and Fair Trade farming has helped cut water consumption on cotton farming by 60%.**

# EMPLOY ME,

## NOT A MACHINE

Developing countries are currently experiencing massive migration from the rural areas to cities because of the steady loss of jobs and livelihoods. In Bangladesh many of these migrants end up as garment factory workers in Dhaka working under exploitative conditions, separated from their families, and living in overcrowded slums. It isn't the bright lights that bring people to the cities, it's hunger. By using hand skills such as hand weaving, hand embroidery and hand knitting we can create employment opportunities for rural artisans, double their income and keep families together.

→ **Hand weaving creates nine times more jobs than running a power loom.**

Hand Loom

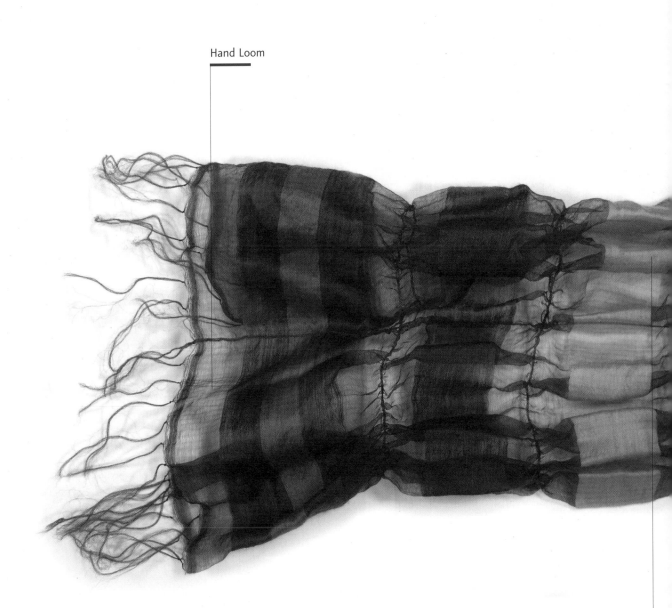

Power Loom

# OUR CARBON
# FOOTPRINT

→ **Taking responsibility for global warming**

People in developing countries have some of the smallest environmental footprints in the world. They live and work in communities without what we would consider the 'essentials' of modern life – a fridge, a washing machine, a car. They buy fewer consumer goods, and eat locally produced food with less packaging. That's why it's unfair that these people are directly threatened by the environmental impact of our buying habits and lifestyles in the West – the pollution from goods manufactured for us and global warming arising from the energy we consume.

→ **Organic farming takes 1 tonne of $CO_2$ per acre per year out of the atmosphere**

→ **Weaving cloth by hand rather than on a machine saves 1 tonne of $CO_2$ emissions each year per handloom.**

→ **CO₂ emissions per head per year**

North America 5.2 tonnes

Eastern Europe 3 tonnes

Western Europe 2.1 tonnes

China 0.6 tonnes

Africa 0.3 tonnes

India 0.2 tonnes

# OVER WASHING

→ 60% of the environmental impact of your clothing comes from washing and caring for them.

→ Washing at 30°C rather than 60°C reduces $CO_2$ emissions per year by enough to fill 4 million double decker buses.

Save the environment, by washing less, washing cold and cooler, wash using environmentally friendly soaps, and drying on a line – you'll save money too!

# People Tree's
## Mission

**To support** producer partners' efforts towards economic independence and control over their environment and to challenge the power structures that undermine their rights to a livelihood.

**To protect** the environment and use natural resources sustainably throughout our trading and to promote environmentally responsible lifestyles and environmental initiatives to create new models to promote sustainability.

**To supply** customers with good quality products, with friendly and efficient service and build awareness to empower consumers and producers to participate in Fair Trade and environmentally sustainable solutions.

**To provide** a supportive environment to all stakeholders and promote dialogue and understanding between them.

**To set an example** to other businesses and the government of a Fair Trade model of business based on partnership, people-centred values and sustainability.

# THE DHAKA

# DECLARATION

This Declaration was put together by Fair Trade producer groups and organisations supporting producer groups making fairly traded garments and handicrafts.

Signatories accept the International Fair Trade Association (IFAT) standards for Fair Trade, along with additional indicators specifically for fashion and textiles. Signatories also recognise certain *Ethical Trade* and *Corporate Social Responsibility* initiatives which highlight issues of illegal, extreme and inhuman working conditions in the fashion industry. Fair Trade therefore sets a *Gold Standard* for Ethical Fashion, guaranteeing the basic legal minimums of Freedom of Association, no enforced overtime, payment of a living wage, health and safety at work etc. And Fair Trade Fashion also goes beyond this – as outlined opposite.

Amid uncertainty in Bangladesh and other countries as to the economic future and stability of the garment industry after the abolition of the MFA in January 2005, Fair Trade projects in rural areas offer producers control over their livelihoods typically through needing less financial capital, ownership structures such as co-operatives or self-employment and through relationships which emphasise the principles of partnership. True Fair Trade offers an alternative economic model which needs to be developed and lobbied for.

**Signatories of the original Dhaka Declaration**

Aarong
Artisan Hut
Folk Bangladesh
GUP
Kumudini Welfare Trust
People Tree
Thanapara Swallows Developr.
Society

**Co-ordination and Drafting Committee of the original Dhaka Declaration, 2004**

Safia Minney
People Tree

Raihan Ali
Thanapara Swallows Developm
Society

Md. Monjurul Haque
Artisan Hut

# Six aims of the
# Dakha declaration

### 1. CREATING JOBS WITHIN COMMUNITIES:
There is an urgent need for livelihoods in many communities, for such reasons as lack of government support, infrastructure and human resources development. Fair Trade provides this efficiently where government policy, businesses and ODA have not yet taken initiatives to support cottage industries e.g handweaving, tailoring and other value-adding to clothing, thus providing an alternative to urban migration, enabling families to stay together and improve their 'real income'. Fair Trade Fashion promotes rural development, ensuring that economic development is recognised.

### 2. CREATING JOBS FOR THE ECONOMICALLY MARGINALISED:
Fair Trade sets out to provide livelihoods for the economically marginalised. Fair Trade clothing has provided thousands of jobs for handweavers, hand embroiderers, block printers and tailors, paying a fair price and helping to provide regular orders, with revenues going back into community development and environmental protection.

### 3. ENCOURAGING GENDER DEVELOPMENT:
Fair Trade clothing production, being very accessible to female producers even when they choose to stay mostly in their home environment, has promoted the empowerment of women as leaders within the community.

### 4. PROMOTING SUSTAINABILITY:
Promoting the use of natural and locally-sourced materials, and environmental production processes.

### 5. PRESERVING TRADITIONAL SKILLS:
Fairly traded clothing is promoting the use of appropriate technology and reviving traditional skills. These products are important to the cultural heritage of the country. These skills create a pride and dignity amongst the producers and within their communities, at the same time as giving economic incentives to develop these skills further. The preservation of these skills have value in themselves that go beyond just economic value.

### 6. PROMOTING FAIR TRADE:
Promoting the Fair Trade Movement and pushing for fairer trade in fashion, our roots are in social justice, community development and member participation and we encourage partnership with movements such as Clean Clothes Campaign and other organisations campaigning for change within the industry.

Natural alpaca yarn is hand spun into bobbins
by indigenous people in the Sierra of Peru.

Silk produced by hand in India, Bangladesh and Laos, providing valuable incomes.

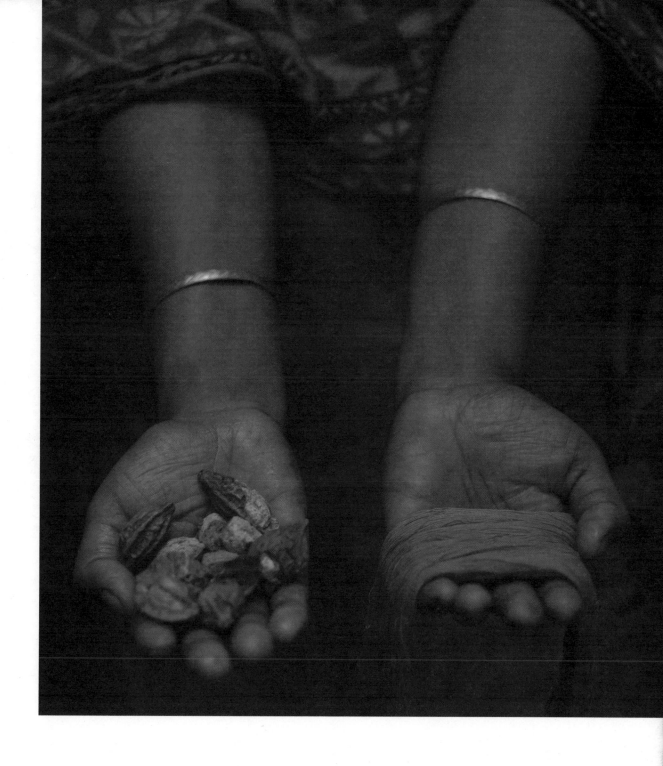

Organic cotton bobbins feed onto a
drum to produce a fine organic cloth.

Reviving natural dye and techniques –
an artisan shows hortoki seeds and dyed
yarn at Swallows, Bangladesh.

Naeem Ansari, dye master, has worked
at Mura collective for ten years.

Mura collective, India was set up to promote natural dyes and shibori tie dye. Naeem shows how the cloth comes out of the indigo vat green before it oxidises, turning blue.

Rinsing off naturally dyed yarn

Shibori tie dye creates unique patterns
at Mura Collective, India

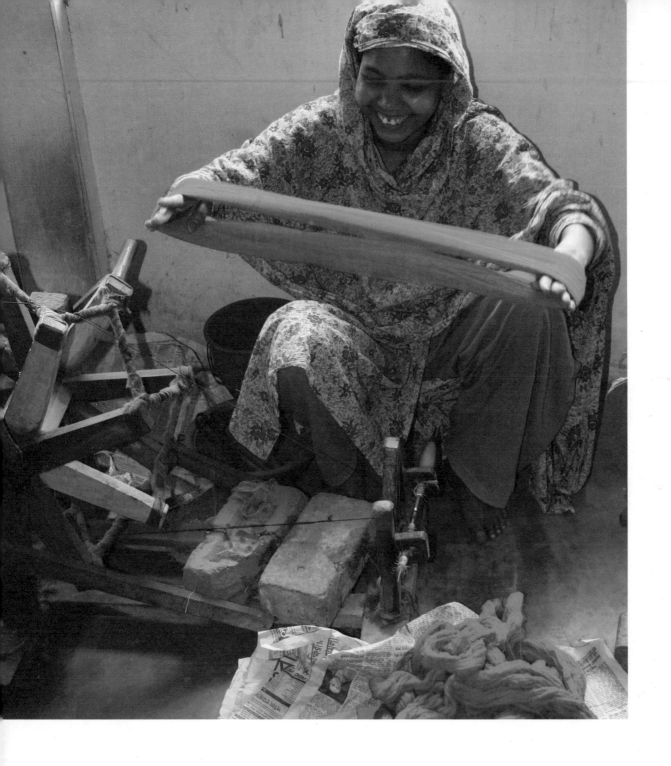

Roksana straightens a hank of yarn before bobbining in preparation for hand weaving.

Ayesha hand weaves at Swallows, Bangladesh producing up to seven metres of cotton cloth each day.

At Brindaban printers, supported by SASHA India, handmade blocks are prepared to print a People Tree chiffon fabric.

A combination of craft skills – traditional hand embroidery: Aari, Ahir, Jat and Kambira from Shrujan-supported groups in the Bhuj area of Gujarat, India.

Batik fabric painting at KVSC, India.

Brindaban Printers hand blocking a
traditional motif in Calcutta, India.

Button making at New Sadle, Nepal. Bone
buttons are individually carved by hand.
All People Tree buttons are made of natural
biodegradable materials like nut, coconut,
shell and bone.

Jhorna stitches a garment at Fair
Trade project Swallows providing
incomes for 150 women.

Suresh Ram presses a People Tree
shirt at Mura Collective, India.

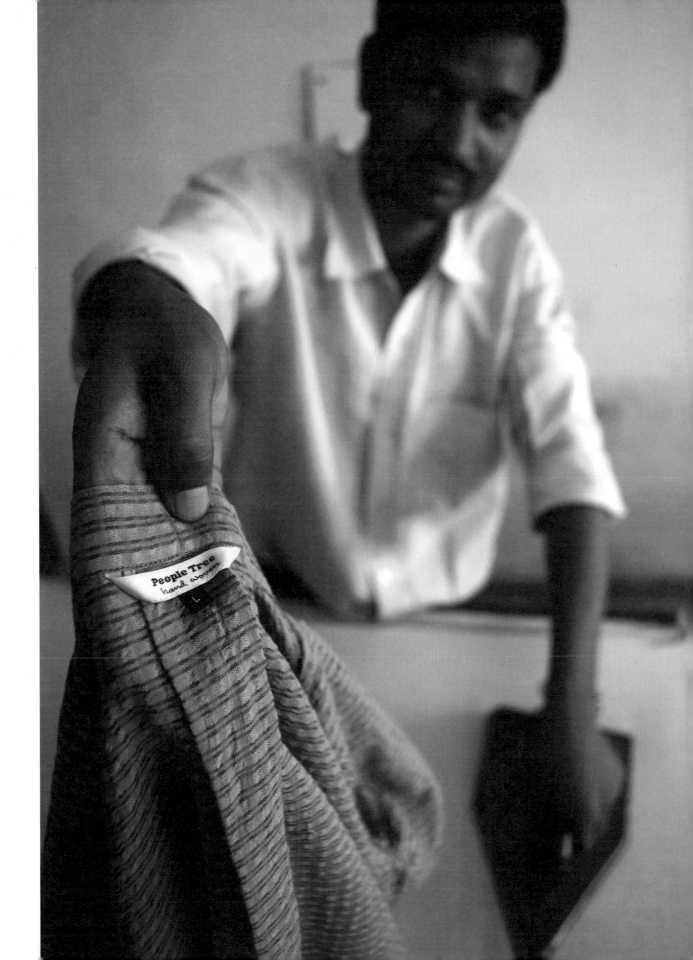

Quechua speaking indigenous women
in Puno, Peru hand spin organic cotton
and alpaca fibres before handknitting
a sweater for People Tree.

Minka has helped communities to
re-introduce quinoa, a highly nutritious
indigenous grain, which is also a very
reliable, resilient crop, helping promote
food security.

Ravu Sunuwar aged 6 says 'Namaste!'
from his school supported by Fair Trade
at Kumbeshwar Technical School, Nepal.

Sunita Giri and Tirtha Tandukar
handknit sweaters and accessories for
People Tree and have doubled their
incomes through Fair Trade.

Mohd Immamudin of Tara Projects
shows a ring design he recently made
for People Tree. Each part of the
decoration is completely made
by hand in India.

Tara Projects and People Tree work
closely together to produce Fair Trade
accessories that are hand crafted and
use natural materials.

# Creating opportunities

## to live and work.

Bombolulu Workshops was established nearly 40 years ago to provide opportunities for people with physical disabilities. It runs Fair Trade production units for jewellery, leatherwork, carving and textiles production, providing work for over 150. Safia Minney talks to Syprine Agan, who has been working at Bombolulu for 18 years.

**SAFIA MINNEY** When did you come to Bombolulu?

**SYPRINE AGAN** 1990, when I was 21. A brother working with a religious organisation in my area of Western Kenya told me about Bombolulu and suggested it would be a good place to be.

**SAFIA** Do you go home to visit your family sometimes?

**SYPRINE** Yes, I travel back to see my family once in a while. It takes about 14 hours by bus from Mombasa. It's far, but it's good to go back and see my family.

**SAFIA** Can you tell me a little more about your childhood and your disability please?

**SYPRINE** I got polio when I was three. I had many brothers and sisters, one surviving brother and three surviving sisters. We had a big family. Where I grew up in the village, my parents were peasant farmers. My mother took me to the dispensary as she noticed my legs were not growing equally. By mistake I was diagnosed with malaria, not polio. Then it was only when I was seven and went for further checks at the district hospital that they realised I had polio and I was given callipers to strengthen and straighten my legs. When the callipers broke we didn't have any money to fix them.

**SAFIA** How did polio affect you growing up?

**SYPRINE** I faced a lot of discrimination; my parents neglected me, favouring my sisters. I went to school until I was 17 and was very strong in maths – that was my favourite subject. Growing up in the village I could do a lot for myself alone and could wash my clothes. Although I wished I could have hung out with my friends and travelled long distances like they did, I could never go far.

**SAFIA** How did your life change when you came to Bombolulu?

**SYPRINE** When I arrived I got training and quickly became skilled at what I do and started earning decently. I got my own home too. Four years ago I married Joseph in our cultural centre. In Kenya when you live together, you say 'come and stay', that's what we did – we lived together first since 2000. I have a son Eugene, who is eleven years old, and Hanna, who is three years old.

I spend $400 US a year on private school fees for Eugene and uniform etc., as the Bombolulu school only goes up to eight years old and the government schools are really poor quality. He really appreciates my working hard to support him to go to a good school.

**SAFIA** How do you spend your Saturdays and Sundays?

**SYPRINE** We go to the beach here in Mombasa. We all love being near the sea.

**SAFIA** How do you think you can increase mobility in Kenya? London is going for 50% wheelchair access in the London Underground for 2012 – what about in developing countries?

**SYPRINE** When you're disabled you have lots of problems getting around. When I have to board a Matatu (local minibus) it is problematic for me with my wheelchair to get on. If disabled people cannot afford to buy and maintain a wheelchair they sometimes have to crawl and this prevents them going to school and work. They cannot fully participate in society. I think this initiative in London is important. General awareness should be higher, so that everyone can move and participate fully in society.

SAFIA Can you imagine life without Bombolulu Workshops?

SYPRINE Bombolulu gave me an opportunity to earn a living and to educate my children. When I am sick I get basic pay but I work on a piece rate basis and work very fast. I earn $4,000 per year which is much higher than the local wages. Sometimes I am in pain because of my disability, but there is help on hand here and respect that comes with doing a good job.

SAFIA You are a specialist in the basket-weave technique, one of the few people who can do this in Kenya – even at Bombolulu. You are the most highly skilled person. How do you feel about this?

SYPRINE I am very happy to hear this. I hope it will bring big orders to our organisation and we will all benefit.

EUGENE I hope my mum will become famous worldwide for her skill!

Syprine with her family.

Syprine makes her basket weave wire bead.

*Fair Trade Fashion –*

---

*a bold statement.*

---

*Handwoven and*

---

*hand-embellished,*

---

*promoting livelihoods*

---

*for rural artisans.*

Photography: Rama
Photographic assistant: Jens Janson
Styling: Kevin Kim
Makeup + Hair: Iwa Park
Model: Sosheba @ Premier

# FAIR TRADE AND
# THE ENVIRONMENT

It is the same system that keeps people poor and destroys the environment. The economic and accounting system we have today only measures financial outcomes, not the social and environmental bottom lines. Our present system rewards short, not long term profit, propelling environmental destruction and widening the gap between rich and poor.

Fair Trade takes a long term view, working in partnership with producers and enabling communities to 'invest' in environmental initiatives and diversify. Organic cotton is grown as a rotational crop alongside organic foods, often consumed by a farmer with the surplus sold locally. Low prices, trade terms and the insecurity that comes from not knowing where your children's next meal will come from push people in the developing world to destroy their environment. After all, why would people whose lives are so dependent on the resources of their natural surroundings, destroy their environment?

Fair Trade, social businesses, and new economics lead the way in showing how we can protect the environment and help the poor feed themselves.

*See www.wftday.org Fair Trade and Environment*

Agrocel works to support over 6,000 cotton
farmers to improve their incomes growing
Fair Trade and organic cotton.

# Farming for

## the future.

Safia Minney talks to Sailesh Patel, Project Manager at Agrocel, about organic cotton farming, the impact of modernisation, the traditional Indian lifestyle and the simple pleasure of sleeping under a neem tree. Agrocel is a Gujarat based organic and Fair Trade farmers' support network that is rapidly expanding throughout India.

SAILESH PATEL I want to congratulate you on writing this book. Lots of people write what they think should happen in the world, but you are writing from your own experiences. It is so very important to document the impact of Fair Trade and organic cotton in India, not just in theory but in practice, so that people can understand how to improve the situation for farmers. This book demonstrates why people should buy Fair Trade and organic cotton and how it makes such a difference.

SAFIA MINNEY Thank you. Much of the activity of your organisation, Agrocel, centres on organic agriculture, growing cotton and rotational crops. Tell me about the additional and subsequent income created through Fair Trade and growing cotton organically, that is, without chemical fertilisers and pesticides?

SAILESH 95% of our farmers are small and tribal farmers working manually, ploughing and harvesting with little or no machinery. Each of the processes is labour intensive and so Fair Trade and organic farming provides maximum employment. Farmers receive up to 30% more money for their cotton when it is organic and Fair Trade. This is particularly important in India where 64% of the population depends on agriculture to make a living. If a farmer uses chemical fertiliser he goes to the nearest shop to buy it and applies it straight to his field, but if he uses manure

it takes two days to prepare. It takes two to two-and-a-half days per acre to plough land with a bullock. Only the big farmers own tractors.

Sowing the seeds manually then takes five to six labourers one day to do. Before the seeds are sown they are coated with organic fertiliser. This coating consists of cow dung, water and fertile soil or bio culture in order to introduce more nitrogen into the soil. Sometimes people use different combinations of cow dung, fermented butter milk, ghee, milk, cow urine and even honey. At Agrocel we never buy seeds from the market, we use our own and cover them with this nutritive coating before planting.

SAFIA And how long does it take to cover one acre of land with organic pesticides?

SAILESH It takes two days to make the pesticides for each acre of land. Neem trees grow locally in the farms. Their leaves and oil are mixed with fermented butter milk, cow urine and water. We use cactus milk to get rid of termites, we chop the acado cactus into small sticks and apply this with the milk from the cactus to the termite hill which is then flooded to kill the termites.

Neem oil – made from crushing seeds from the trees – is diluted and used as a spray. We use 20 millilitres of neem oil for every

66

litre of water and the fields are sprayed four to five times during each crop. There are many natural ways to control pests and strengthen the eco system so that it is more able to take care of itself.

**SAFIA** In India the population is increasing and people's hands are literally the most valuable resource the country has. Do you think that if we adopt organic and Fair Trade agriculture we can generate enough employment for everyone? Enough to put food on the table of every household and provide basic education and healthcare for all?

**SAILESH** For many years India has been dependent on agriculture, it's how most people earn their living. Many cotton farmers not growing good crops are using expensive fertilisers and pesticides. There is a desperate need to do things differently and improve the situation for the farmers. With proper planning and development activities like Fair Trade we can change this. Organic farming creates much more employment than conventional farming.

**SAFIA** Many people are now returning to live in the Gujarat area, why is that?

**SAILESH** The government has provided electricity, good roads and communications in the village and drip irrigation. People have new income opportunities. Better infrastructure encourages farmers to come back to the villages for work.

**SAFIA** So do you think all this development is sustainable? Do you think that basic food, education and infrastructure for transport and additional provisions such as health care and further education will satisfy today's Indian people? The new so-called low cost car, Tata Nano – a tiny, four door, four seat hatchback – costs around £1,000 in India. Is there a danger that people will want goods like this and want to keep consuming more, as they have done in the west, because clearly the western model does not add up. What's your vision for India?

**SAILESH** We have good public transportation to the towns. Our area has a population of 1,000 people, they do not need cars

and are not interested in them. Transportation infrastructure developments allow people to get where they need to go. If these links are good enough, people – even the more wealthy – do not need cars.

Indian culture is different. Living in large families, living in the village, means that they are more connected with each other. For example, each Sunday my local barber comes to my home to cut hair and give my father, my cousins and I, a shave. He does a very good job. When we have ceremonies, like my marriage ceremony, he comes and joins us for dinner or for lunch. There is a common understanding that life is like this, he is like a family doctor. He is very much connected to the community, he goes to six or seven families like this. If he has a problem with his health or something like that, we have a responsibility to look after him. This relationship has been there for generations. We give him presents during festivals. Each year we give grain and money to those who need it.

**SAFIA** How is modernisation affecting these traditional aspects of village life?

**SAILESH** It's not all good. Toothpaste is an example of modernisation. Around 1,000 people are employed by toothpaste-making factories. We used to use neem and bamboo sticks that were made by families of the lowest caste – 20,000 to 30,000 people who nowadays have no work. Now only old people use the sticks. And of course plastic toothbrushes are not biodegradable, unlike a neem or bamboo stick.

**SAFIA** Why have Agrocel been so supportive of People Tree's other Fair Trade partners, helping to promote handweaving with organic cotton and helping us to start an organic cotton project in Bangladesh?

**SAILESH** There are many examples of how hand production helps communities. Our company wants to help not only the farmers but the workers, weavers, dyers and embroidery artisans. There has been a bitter modernisation cycle in India. It should be Fair Trade on both sides – if it is just farmers who benefit it is a relatively small return, but if you add hand production, thousands more can stand to gain.

Power loom factories ask to buy our cotton, I prioritise the handloom first. So much work has gone into the cotton and I do not want to give it to factories with machines. I am passionate about creating livelihoods in handweaving.

I have studied economics so I know the difference that hand skills make. I talked to the women at the khadi units and they told me how thankful they are for being given the opportunity to work with handweaving projects, it makes a real difference. The 800 handlooms in the Calcutta Khadi project provide around 1,000 people with employment.

Agrocel is very interested in sustainability and development. Handweaving does not damage the environment; handlooms do not give off $CO_2$, unlike machine looms do through burning oil – another reason why it is so important to support these kinds of hand skills.

SAFIA If Gandhi – who struggled for the independence of India throughout his life – had been sitting next to you at the People Tree Fair Trade fashion show you watched today, what do you think he would have thought?

SAILESH It is very difficult to answer such a question. If Gandhi saw that the clothes had been made by hand by Indian people, maybe he would be proud. And maybe he would think that if more Indian people worked in this way, it would help towards solving the problems they face.

SAFIA What would happen if India was to follow the western model of development? Particularly considering global warming and the oil crisis.

SAILESH If our culture develops like the West's then we would have a big problem. But the Indian model is different as we have our own traditions and skills. India is in between and can go back to a simpler way of life. We know how to use natural resources properly and appropriately. We do not require much energy in the village. For example, in small villages farmers use bullocks for energy, not machinery, and can grow enough food for themselves to live quite comfortably.
The Indian way of life is very simple. My father and I used to go into the nearest town about once every 15 days with everything we wanted to take in cloth bags, no plastic.

Many small, local businesses gathered there to trade with each other. We would go in the morning, travel by cart, taking our products to sell: peanuts, grain, cotton and excess crops. We would return home that evening, with any extra things we needed. At home, we crushed peanuts to make oil and the rice and vegetables that we grew were sufficient for our needs.

SAFIA How have things changed for farmers in India?

SAILESH The farmers know agriculture and have the skills to farm. But modernisation has come along and tried to impose methods that use lots of natural resources like water, and chemical fertilisers and pesticides which ultimately make the soil less fertile. This modernisation has taught the farmers bad practices that are not sustainable. Even though it is farmers who supply food for the world, the west keeps telling farmers what to do and when it doesn't work out as planned the farmers suffer the consequences.

SAFIA How will Agrocel spread the benefits of organic and Fair Trade farming practices to more farmers?

SAILESH Agrocel is expanding its Fair Trade and organic networks into Orissa and the southern states, so our work is now in five states, including in the south in Andhra Pradesh, Karnataka and Tamil Nadu. Many people now come to us asking for advice on how to set up projects like ours. Maybe one day we will help African farmers too.

SAFIA Would it help to set up a carbon credits programme for farmers? Per acre Agrocel is already reducing one and a half tonnes of carbon dioxide emissions per acre, per year through organic farming methods and there are 15,000 acres across the network. At today's rate of around £15 per tonne of $CO_2$, that would make over £40,000 per year. Surely a sum that large could help to train more farmers in the importance of protecting the environment?

SAILESH Yes, but it is still not enough because the farmer is the one that suffers first from global warming. If his crops fail because of drought then he does not get any income and will go hungry. Farmers are now calling for those who live in urban areas in the developing countries to take more personal

responsibility for the impact of their lifestyles.

It is best if people simply use less. Resources, like water and energy, should be used appropriately. By being vegetarian we would be helping nature and the farmers, by promoting agriculture and saving energy. If you calculate how much energy we use to produce one kilogramme of meat compared to the same quantity of a vegetable, the vegetable uses far less energy. We should also develop a system for people to live within their own resources, in Mumbai many hotels throw more than a tonne of food each day away and yet more than 1,000 people in the city go to sleep hungry each night.

SAFIA Tell me about the things that make you happy.

SAILESH In India we believe that happiness does not come from having money or possessions. Happiness is in helping each other and living together. All the world is one family – everyone helps each other and that makes happiness for all.

SAFIA You told me recently that sometimes you sleep under the neem tree – a real pleasure that money can't buy!

SAILESH Yes, when it's really hot I sleep under the neem tree in our family garden. It uses no energy and is a wonderful restorative. I recommend it!

*From its 12 rural service centres across India, Agrocel co-ordinates organic and Fair Trade agriculture and capacity building for farmers' organisations. Agrocel's partnership with People Tree has been essential in creating a complete supply chain for certified organic textile products in India, and Agrocel is generously providing technical expertise for doing the same for Bangladesh.*

*The bright side –*

*not only Fair Trade*

*cotton fibre,*

*but 100% organic*

*certified and*

*Fair Trade*

*manufactured*

*too.*

Photography + Styling: Annoushka Giltsoff
Model: Renne @ Storm

# FAIR TRADE
# STANDARDS

## 1

## *Creating opportunities*

## *for economically disadvantaged*

## *producers*

Fair Trade is a strategy for poverty alleviation and sustainable development. Its purpose is to create opportunities for producers who have been economically disadvantaged or marginalised by the conventional trading system.

## 2

## *Transparency and*

## *accountability*

Fair Trade involves transparent management and commercial relations to deal fairly and respectfully with trading partners.

## 3
# Capacity building

Fair Trade is a means to develop producers' independence. Fair Trade relationships provide continuity, during which producers and their marketing organisations can improve their management skills and their access to new markets.

## 4
# Promoting Fair Trade

Fair Trade organisations raise awareness of Fair Trade and the possibility of greater justice in world trade. They provide their customers with information about the organisation, the products, and in what conditions they are made. They use honest advertising and marketing techniques and aim for the highest standards in product quality and packing.

## 5
# Payment of a fair price

A fair price in the regional or local context is one that has been agreed through dialogue and participation. It covers not only the costs of production but enables production which is socially just and environmentally sound. It provides fair pay to the producers and takes into account the principle of equal pay for equal work by women and men. Fair Traders ensure prompt payment to their partners and, whenever possible, help producers with access to pre-harvest or pre-production financing.

# 6

# *Gender equity*

Fair Trade means that women's work is properly valued and rewarded.
Women are always paid for their contribution to the production process
and are empowered in their organisations.

# 7

# *Working conditions*

Fair Trade means a safe and healthy working environment for producers. The
participation of children (if any) does not adversely affect their well-being,
security, educational requirements and need for play and conforms to the UN
Convention on the Rights of the Child as well as the law in the local context.

# 8

# *Child labour*

Fair Trade Organisations respect the UN Convention on the Rights of the
Child, as well as local laws and social norms in order to ensure that the
participation of children in production processes of fairly traded articles
(if any) does not adversely affect their well-being, security, educational
requirements and need for play. Organisations working directly with
informally organised producers disclose the involvement of children
in production.

## 9
# *The environment*

Fair Trade actively encourages better environmental practices and the application of responsible methods of production.

## 10
# *Trade relations*

Fair Trade organisations trade with concern for the social, economic and environmental well-being of marginalised small producers and do not maximise profit at their expense. They maintain long-term relationships based on solidarity, trust and mutual respect that contribute to the promotion and growth of Fair Trade. Whenever possible producers are assisted with access to pre-harvest or pre-production advance payment.

## IFAT – International Fair Trade Association

IFAT's mission is to improve the livelihoods and well-being of disadvantaged producers by linking and promoting Fair Trade organisations, and speaking out for the greater justice in world trade. More than 265 members in 60 countries across the world have come together in solidarity and mutual co-operation to create an alternative and fairer way of doing business. People Tree joined IFAT in 1996.

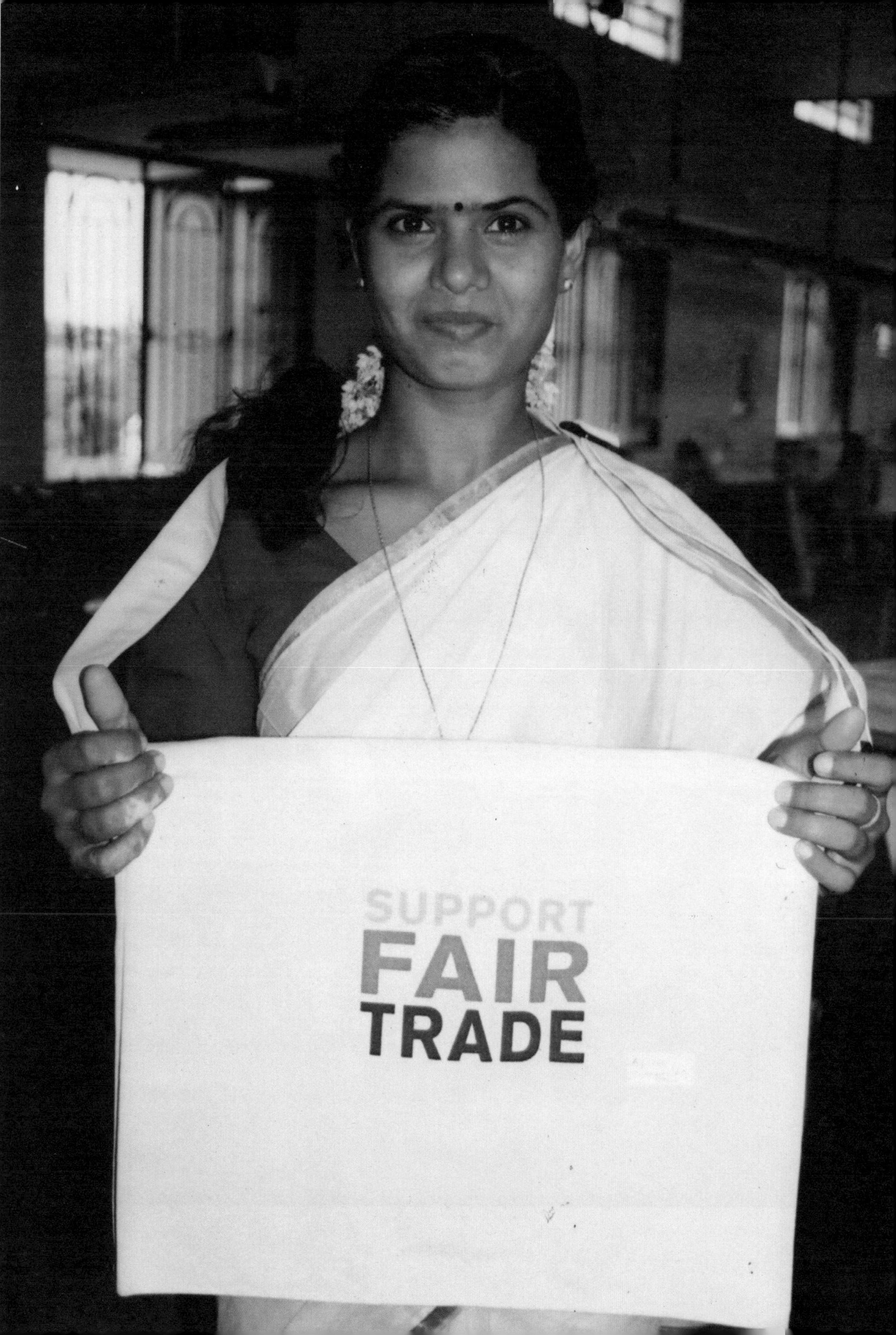
SUPPORT
FAIR
TRADE

# CAMPAIGNING

# FOR CHANGE

Fair Trade is more than just a fair deal for people in the developing world. It is an international movement bringing the voice of the poor to the forefront. We raise public awareness, talk to business and policy makers about what's happening around the world and campaign for people's rights.

Fair Trade campaigns for human rights and environmental justice and against the structural causes of poverty. The truth is that companies often use the 'opportunity' of people's economic poverty and voicelessness to exploit them, grab their land and its natural resources, and pollute their environment.

Even where legislation exists, it is often not enforced. Despite our governments having signed the International Labour Organisation (ILO) conventions to protect workers with a minimum wage and health and safety standards, hundreds lose their lives or are injured in garment factory fires each year. Retailers and brands on our high streets often abuse the minimum wage and working conditions, resulting in families unable to feed themselves adequately. Likewise, the World Health Organisation (WHO) agreement to ban the use of toxic and hazardous chemicals is constantly ignored by seed and chemical multinationals and undermined by agricultural policy. This has affected the health and physical development of children and destroys traditional farming practices. This has indirectly led to more than 100,000 farmer suicides in India in the last 10 years alone, due to debts arising from misguided purchases of unnecessary products.

As the 'race to the bottom' accelerates, with ever lower prices that don't cover social and environmental costs, short delivery times, and bad terms of trade – our planet and its people are being pushed to the edge.

Fair Trade shows that there is a different way of doing business, by working in close partnership to help people escape from poverty and protect the environment. The problem is that the rest of the world doesn't know this yet. That's because there are huge vested interests in keeping the world from knowing, getting angry, and changing the way we do business.

That's why People Tree campaigns for farmers' and workers' rights, a fairer trading and economic system, corporate accountability and protection of the environment. We work with the media and like-minded organisations like *Pesticide Action Network* and *War on Want*. We are at the forefront of the Fair Trade movement, and in 2002 initiated World Fair Trade Day which is endorsed by IFAT (International Fair Trade Association).

We believe good sense will prevail. After all, most people want to do the right thing. We all know that a dysfunctional society and environmental destruction will affect us all.

Chemical pesticides and genetically modified
seeds can lead the farmer into inexorable
cycles of debt and poverty.

Stop the Lethal Use of "Dirty Dozen" WHO-banned Chemicals in Developing Countries

At the 6th World Trade Organisation Ministerial Conference in Hong Kong in December 2006, we developed the Cotton Position Paper with friends in the Fair Trade movement. This called for a stop to the $3 billion subsidies which the US gives its large-scale cotton farmers. This subsidy artificially keeps the international price of cotton 25% lower, making it increasingly difficult for developing country cotton farmers to earn a living wage. We launched it with a Fair Trade fashion show, opened by the Indian Minister for Trade and Commerce, Kamal Nath, and it was on the front page of the newspapers the next day. Today's economic system and policy largely serves the rich and multinational corporate interests because the poor have such a small voice and no platform. Together we can help them make their voices heard.

We haven't solved the problem yet, so read more on
www.peopletree.co.uk/positionpaperoncotton.php

# Sweatshops

## Why are products so cheap? Do the brands you buy protect the human rights of the people who make their clothing?

In 1998 People Tree and Global Village launched a campaign to raise awareness of garment factory workers' situation and put pressure on high street retailers to change their ways. As part of our research, we had long been visiting workers in their homes in the slums in Bangladesh and India, and gone into their factories incognito to find out what Fair Trade fashion was fairer than. The reality is that workers could rarely earn enough to afford to feed themselves 2,000 calories a day, despite extremely physical 14-hour days with only 2 days off a month. Typically, two to three adults will share a 'home' the space of the average British bathroom, with up to 30 such 'homes' sharing a 'kitchen' of three or four burners. The same number of households share one toilet, and a shower.

The cost of living is on average three times higher than in the rural areas, and with no extended family on hand, and no small plot to grow vegetables or keep chickens, factory workers are incredibly isolated and out of touch with their roots. It isn't the bright lights that brought these people to the factories and the slums that surround them; it is the need to feed their hungry families. Asked if they would prefer, if they could, to work in rural areas, there was a resounding 'Yes'.

This level of exploitation is a consequence of the low prices the high street chains pay for garments and the short delivery times that conventional fashion insists on.

安いモノは、なぜ安い？
あなたの好きなブランドは
つくる人の権利を守っていますか。

**FREEDOM** of association
組合結成の自由

**RIGHT** to collective bargaining
団体交渉の権利

**NO** forced labour
強制労働の禁止

**NO** child labour
児童労働の禁止

**NO** discrimination
差別の禁止

Maximum **HOURS** of work
労働時間の規定

**HEALTH** and **SAFETY**
安全と衛生の確保

**A LIVING WAGE**
最低賃金の保障

**SECURITY** of employment
安定した雇用の保障

GLOBAL VILLAGE     **People Tree**

# Child labour – a fact of the fashion industry.

We work with Fair Trade partner, Tara Projects. Being half Indian myself, I am able to move in the slums and workshops of old Delhi quite freely. Hundreds of children as young as 8, often bonded labourers, make jewellery and trinket boxes for the big British brands.

Whether it's working in a cotton field or a ginnery, beadwork embroidery on T shirts, or accessories, products made by children hang in our high street stores. Why? Because children will work for a third of the wages that adults do – and consumers want the cheapest prices while companies want to maximise profits. Another cause of child labour is economic policy that takes livelihoods away from their parents – leaving them little choice but to watch their family go hungry, or send their child away to work.

There are nearly 200 million children trapped in child labour. Of those, nearly half are in hazardous work. Recently, initiatives in developing countries have been successful in focussing on mass education, to move children from the workplace to school, and educate society that the child has the right not to work – but more needs to be done. Fair Trade and NGOs worldwide spearhead a worldwide movement to change policy, hold companies accountable for child labour, and improve adult working conditions.

Typically, in a single workshop, 12 boys between the ages of 8 and 16 will work for 14–16 hours daily, eat and sleep in a room the size of the average British lounge. They earn as little as £4 per month and are often brutalised. The only recreation they have is to watch TV whilst eating their supper. Who is to blame? The owner of the workshop employing the children, or the customer who wants cheap products? Clearly it is both, and the middlemen between them. The workshop owners were often child labourers themselves and are uneducated, trapped competing with each other on price and delivery times. Then there are the agents, traders and buyers, who vie for the cheapest prices to supply the high street. But we cannot simply take work away from child labourers and abandon them. Some progressive companies and Fair Trade organisations campaign for fair wages for adults and against child labour, at the same time as starting schools for child labourers, that allow them time for work. For an example, see 'Chamomile Children' in www.sekem.com/english/cultural/Foundation.aspx?PageID=5.

Fair Trade, by paying a fair price and working in long term partnership with adults, ensures that parents can send their children to school. The Fair Trade movement is against child labour, but it is not against child work. Child work offers the child the opportunity to help their family, build self-esteem and learn skills, whilst going to school and having some time to have fun with friends. Perhaps a better balance than the TV and gaming youth of the so-called developed world.

*Fair fashion means fabric and manufacture that promote quality of life and preserve skills and the environment.*

Photography: Boo Kyoung Lee
Stylist: Anders Soelvsten
Make up + Hair Stylist: Sunghee Park
Model: Joleen @ Quintessentially

# Clothes for
# the soul.

Safia Minney talks to Kusum Tiwari, founder of Mura Collective in Delhi, about the intangible happiness of wearing handwoven fabrics, healing properties of natural dyes and training crafts-people to benefit society as a whole.

SAFIA MINNEY What drove you to work in handcrafts in Delhi?

KUSUM TIWARI In India today we have a huge population but many people do not have any work. There are so many hands and feet that could work – the biggest asset India has!

Each machine-powered loom that is in operation takes work away from these many willing hands. This results in a vicious cycle of poverty, starvation and eventually even suicide. The people should be producing something: crafts, textiles, growing crops, working in agriculture. But mechanisation, science for that matter, is not supporting society. Humankind has invented so many things and made so many discoveries that support humanity in its journey, but in today's world, science is taking away human rights.

The mind is given to us as a tool to use. If we use it constructively, the body remains positive. But if we allow the mind to take over, it becomes destructive. Tools – like our minds, machines and even computers – can support what we do, but in today's world they seem to have become an end in themselves.

SAFIA In India today the handweaving industry employs millions of people, it is second only to agriculture and one of the most robust economies in India. From the income that these handweavers now receive for their

craft work they have been able to provide for their families. Given that handweaving as an industry is so huge and providing income for so many, is there enough being done to support hand weaving cottage industries in India and internationally?

KUSUM The most supportive action that consumers can take is to buy the products that are produced by these millions of people, in fact that's the only support they get. The materials being made are being compared to machine woven fabrics, when the only comparable elements are the texture and quality of the fabric. With a handloom fabric there is a very subtle quality that's not really tangible, it's the energy of the hand that has made it.

SAFIA How can the consumer recognise, or feel the energy that is brought to handloom fabric?

KUSUM Personally, I only wear handloom fabric, I will not wear anything that is not made by hand. If ever I dress myself in a fabric that is not made by hand, immediately I'll find that it is not comfortable. The energy of the fabric is not something that will be able to be assessed in conventional terms, unless science gives us the technology to measure the energy of a person and how it alters after wearing a handloom fabric. It is a subtle sense of happiness, a great comfort level that you derive from products that are made by hand.

**SAFIA** Is it literally the energy of the weaver that is left in the garment that creates this feeling of wellbeing, rather than the feelgood factor that comes from being part of a solution that supports people's economic independence?

**KUSUM** Well it is always both, the universe always works like this. A person buys a product and they receive the energy of its maker and the knowledge that they are contributing to the maker's livelihood and therefore their wellbeing. So the giver is also the receiver.

**SAFIA** Why did you leave your job as a software engineer to start Mura Collective?

**KUSUM** I wanted to work more with women. I am not a feminist but in all cultures, in some way or other, this universe has been motivated by power and by getting more out of other people. Most of the women who come to other people's homes in India to work – to cook or clean or wash clothes – are really struggling. A woman is naturally a nurturer and she wants to give. And while some men are very sensitive and very supportive, most do not nurture their families as women do. In India often you'll find that if the man works he will spend his wages on himself, on drinking, or on his friends. Unfortunately many men just don't want to work and they don't want to contribute to support their families. And we found that husbands did not trust their wives to go into workplaces that were run by men, so we have had to build up their confidence by starting them at work at Mura.

**SAFIA** Do the women that you train already have craft skills?

**KUSUM** We teach them the skills. For the past seven years we have taught a lot of women the art of 'shibori' (tie dye). Each woman has been taught the basic stitch and refined it almost to perfection. They then take this basic skill and develop it themselves. Unfortunately we can only work with 30 to 40 women at a time, but we have trained close to 150 women over the years. We teach them other skills too, like using natural dyes, so that they can get work in other organisations in the area and stay close to their families.

**SAFIA** What sparked your interest in using natural dyes?

**KUSUM** I met a man at an art gallery who was about 90 years old and I was infected by his passion, he had so much love for natural dyes and that inspired the Mura Collective's interest. We experimented using regular household materials. Turmeric, for example, gives a beautiful colour, but it was not very colour-fast. Onions turned fabric pink and we used tea for a beautiful light brown colour. We also use natural indigo dye for a lot of work.

**SAFIA** What is the relevance of natural dyes in contemporary clothing? We hear of the healing properties of some materials, for example, the cooling effects of indigo – were you interested in that too?

**KUSUM** We started off using natural dyes simply because they made us happy in the same way that wearing handloom fabrics makes you happy – we love natural dyes! One might momentarily be attracted to synthetic dyes, but there is nothing behind the colour, so the happiness doesn't last. When you wear natural dyed fabric it gives you a special feeling. Nature has made everything so perfect.

*Mura Collective provides work for 60 handweavers, natural dyers and tailors in Delhi, India.*

# VOGUE JAPAN
# COLLABORATIONS

"*Thanks to People Tree and its producers, we have been able to show the fashion industry that Fair Trade fashion can be cool. I hope this is just the start of a global movement towards fashion with a conscience!*"
— Leeyong Soo, International Fashion Coordinator for Vogue NIPPON

Leeyong came to see us at the People Tree Japan office – and we brainstormed over a cup of Fair Trade coffee. Wouldn't it be great if we could link up with some of the hottest international designers to promote People Tree's work and raise awareness of just how desirable Fair Trade Fashion could be?

We sent our project proposal letters to 15 or so carefully selected designers and within a few weeks Bora Aksu, Richard Nicoll, Thakoon and Foundation Addict agreed not only to work with People Tree producers' handwoven, hand embellished, organic fabrics, but also to have 200 of each outfit tailored in our Fair Trade projects in Bangladesh and India. People Tree technicians and designers helped pattern cutters and tailors and the results were stunning.

In celebration of World Fair Trade Day 2007, Vogue's June issue featured Fair Trade Fashion at its best. Helena Christensen wore Bora Aksu's organic and Fair Trade certified dress with recycled sari sash belt, Lily Cole wore Thakoon's handwoven dress, Anne Watanabe wore Richard Nicoll's handwoven shirt, and Shalom Harlow wore Foundation Addict's 3-piece organic handwoven waistcoat, shorts and shirt. Fair Trade Fashion had arrived – it was no longer a story about Fair Trade foods alone, and the ripples were felt through the fashion world in Japan. In the UK too, it was a turning point, with coverage in over 20 fashion magazines and general press too.

"*I'm so happy with the way it turned out. The sleeve is quite complicated, so I imagined at first that it would become a problem – but actually the sleeve work came out beautifully. A couture-like sleeve was no problem!*"
— Thakoon, designer

Bora Aksu
Bora Aksu

も、チャリティーのためにリサイク
オでドレスを作った」と語るボラは、
ドンをベースにしているトルコ人、
ドにある障害者や貧困家庭の女性を
するグループ、「アシシ・ガーメン
で制作したオーガニックコットンの
ピースに、女性の経済力や地位の向
目指して活動している「サシャ」と
団体が作った一点一点が違うリサイ
・サリーベルトを合わせて、「現代
インにおいてフェアトレードは無関
と思ってたけど、これからも機会が
ば参加したいと思ったわ」と誇る。

Helena Christensen
ナ・クリステンセン

パーモデルとして有名になったヘレ
現在フォトグラファーとして活躍中。
カファッション誌や広告キャンペー
活躍し、パリのコレットなどで展覧
開かれたことも。また、「Butik」とい
レクトショップをニューヨークで経
さまざまなチャリティに関わる中、
ルノブイリ事故で苦しむ子どもの助
なる、Chernobyl Children's Project
national を積極的にサポートしている。
www.chernobyl-international.org/

o: Helena Christensen

Aksu for People Tree　サリーベル
き OCパネルドレス ¥25,000 ／ ピ
ル・ツリー　スニーカー、ソックス、
クレス、ブレスレット／すべてモデ
物

ORGANIC COTTON DEMONSTRATION
VARIETY: DEVIRAJ
SEED FROM: RAPAR
SOWING DATE: 20 AUGUST, 07
ORGANIC COTTON PROJECT, FAIR TRADE CO. JAPAN

## Thakoon

New York based Thakoon has collaborated with People Tree to design these gorgeous pieces in 100% organic and Fair Trade jersey cotton, handwoven cotton and silks. Thakoon is one of the most influential designers in the world, famous for mixing ethereal looks with urban to create pieces worn by Sarah Jessica Parker and Demi Moore.

**Richard Nicoll**

People Tree first worked with Richard Nicoll last summer on a collaboration with Vogue Japan to show that Fair Trade fashion can also be high fashion. Richard has been showing at London Fashion week since 2006. He is renowned for his beautiful yet incredibly wearable clothes, particularly shirts. Richard designed this flamboyantly ruffled collar shirt for People Tree using hand woven fabrics made by Folk Bangladesh. Folk work with ethnic minority hand weavers and embroiderers around Bangladesh.

Fair Trade hand-knit cardigan
for Topshop

Bora Aksu for People
Tree check dress, sold
exclusively by ASOS
and People Tree.

Sam Ubhi bracelet
Autumn / Winter 2008

*Tatami Japan,*
*a Birkenstock brand*

# Designer
## collaborations

Safia Minney talks to Bora Aksu about his passion for Fair Trade fashion and his latest collaboration with People Tree.

**SAFIA MINNEY** How is working with People Tree different to doing your own collection?

**BORA AKSU** For our own show we only finish everything one month before the show, so to meet the long lead times in this project, we need to be a lot more organised. I'm really happy with the results and I think it is amazing what you are doing to provide livelihoods for these people, but it isn't a one way thing – they are providing you with amazing hand work and finishing too.

The garments that we were just looking at today have a really drapey feel and the finishing on them was amazing. I never thought this would be possible with Fair Trade but the more I work with People Tree, the more I learn about these things.

**SAFIA** Have you always chosen the materials you use in your collection carefully, even before you started working with People Tree?

**BORA** Most of the fabrics we conventionally use are from Italy and for my designs I only use natural fabrics like 100% wools and 100% silks. There are different textures but the base materials are always silks, cottons or wools.

I was really excited about using People Tree's handwoven and hand dyed fabrics, and your pure silks and cottons. It wasn't like 'we have this fabric and must use it', it was more like excitement because these fabrics were so beautiful, and also similar to those I use for my own collections. It was great to create something with fabric that I am very familiar with. I believe that fashion has a unique and international language; the garment that you

produce has to be desirable for the customer so it doesn't matter if it's Fair Trade or organic, or this or that. If the customer is not attracted to the garment then they won't buy it. So my whole concept is to attract the customer, to make the clothing desirable – and I think it's working really well between us.

**SAFIA** I am really interested to know why you love natural and handwoven materials. For me it used to be all about poverty alleviation and environmental issues but now I see it more politically. We are running out of oil, we are going to war for oil; we are running out of water, there are communities experiencing huge conflicts because of water. With the population going from 6 billion to 9-10 billion in the next 30 years, the only natural energy source we have is people's hands. Natural and hand crafted fabrics bring Fair Trade and environmental justice together. Is this an answer for sustainable fashion? Could it scale up? Could we actually do a Gandhian thing?

**BORA** I don't think raising awareness overnight is going to happen, but projects and collaborations like ours raise awareness. It starts through the press then people became more and more interested. It brings that question mark to mind when people are buying a garment, to ask themselves 'where is this coming from?'. I myself am very against things that are really fashionable. If people are asking where a garment has come from, and about the real cost of a garment, things will change.

People have a mindset that Fair Trade is very expensive and that it is difficult to find what you want. I think it takes a long time, but with products like this you can change people's minds.

SAFIA What motivates you? Is it the handwoven and handcrafted fabrics, or that thousands of women increase their incomes by 50%, and that premiums paid from Fair Trade products help to fund a school for 600 children, and other social and environmental projects to bring benefits to the wider community?

BORA I think it's amazing, not talking as a designer but as a human being. It is the individual's responsibility to make these kinds of choices. It should not only be through People Tree or only through this collaboration – it should be a responsibility that everyone carries with them.

SAFIA For your own collection or when you are designing for People Tree, who is your muse?

BORA You.

SAFIA Ha ha ha ha – very sweet thing to say but really?

BORA No, I think I design for friends and people around me. I design for real people, but the thing is, when you are actually creating for a fashion show it is different; you are almost creating an imaginary world.

I quite like how people wear items from my collections with their own clothes, like wearing an evening dress with their denim and adding a more personal touch. That is what people do when they buy from a shop. They buy something and then they wear it with their own stuff, giving it their own mark.

That's why I like it when people wear my clothes and they wear it with their own belt, their own styling – it is something that I designed but they make it their own. In fact when I was designing this collection with People Tree that was my concept, the clothes need to have a wider aspect so people can wear the jacket over an evening dress, or denim, or a t-shirt. It should give ideas to people, they almost start doing their own design through buying these garments and making them their own. I think that is how you come to buy a garment – you see yourself in it and wearing it with your own things.

SAFIA Do you think good design can be timeless, that there can be longevity? Can design last forever?

"I think it's amazing, not talking as a designer but as a human being. It is the individual's responsibility to make these kinds of choices."

BORA I think so yes. I think things have changed a lot. In the 90s it was more the fashion houses and designers that were dictating to people. I think people have changed a lot since then and if you look at the trends now it is more about 'what I want'. It is almost like there is something for everyone; you can find baggy clothes, you can find fitted clothes. I think people are more aware of their individual tastes. They want to search for things that they like, still following trends to a certain degree but also their own personal style.

SAFIA So you think people have a more individual look, one they are developing and evolving?

BORA Yes, and that this is how it should be. I don't think it should be designers or companies deciding how people should look, almost brainwashing them through the press, magazines and on TV so that they think 'this is how we should look, this is how I should dress to fit into society'. I think women are not thinking like that so much anymore.

SAFIA Where would you like to see the Bora Aksu for People Tree collections sold in the future?

BORA I think it is going in the right direction. From a really high end customer to a customer that just wants to follow trends or fashion, I think they can all find something in our collaboration, and it will make people more open minded about Fair Trade. I would like to see the People Tree designer collections in all the high end stores such as Selfridges and Barneys, because the collection is strong enough to be in those stores.

SAFIA Finally, if you were to visit one of our producers, which would you most like to visit?

**BORA** I would love to visit the Bangladesh ones especially Swallows. I would absolutely love to go there.

**SAFIA** You're on! They would love to meet you too, to thank you personally for all your support.

**Bora Aksu**

Bora Aksu debuted at London Fashion Week in 2003 after graduating from the fashion MA at Central Saint Martins with a distinction. He has won the Topshop New Generation award three times. People Tree first worked with Bora last summer in a collaboration with Vogue Japan.

The layered dress and tunic are characteristics of Bora's signature with feminine, floaty and sexy shapes. They have been produced by People Tree's partner, Folk Bangladesh, a group that employs 550 artisans from marginalised communities. These are complicated patterns so they were a challenge, but all of us are thrilled with the results.

# Creatives for change.

Safia Minney talks to Chris Haughton, illustrator and creative mind behind some great People Tree graphics and messages.

Did you know...

more pesticides are used on cotton than any other crop.

In developed countries this has been recognised to be extremely harmful and many cotton pesticides have been banned.

But in developing countries pesticide is difficult to regulate as cotton farmers are amongst the poorest in the world...

In India cotton crops use 54% of all pesticides...

...and yet cotton is grown on just 5% of all arable land.

At People Tree we have been supporting small scale farmers groups and helping them convert to less harmful practices.

Thank you for supporting our organic cotton growers....

# People Tree
fair trade organic cotton

You can see the full animation at - http://uk.youtube.com/watch?v=6P3Y1ZrWhvM&feature=related

**SAFIA** How long have you been working with People Tree? What motivated you to use your creativity to promote Fair Trade and environmental issues?

**CHRIS** I've been working with People Tree for four years. I had wanted to become involved in the Fair Trade movement since travelling in India and Nepal for a summer while I was in college. It was a very eye opening trip. When I left I was a fairly apathetic art student, but I was so dumbfounded by the poverty that by the time I came back I was reading all these books on economics. I found it very difficult to understand how such hardworking people could be so poor.

**SAFIA** Why did you get fed up working in the conventional creative industry, and want to design for social change as well?

**CHRIS** As a designer, to keep myself interested and passionate I always really try to put full effort into the work I do. I had been working with some big companies and did some quite high profile jobs but ultimately I felt I was wasting my time in design and advertising when it came down to it. It was very superficial and mostly the people I worked for only cared about sales, money and the position of their logo. They weren't small companies so I didn't care much whether they sold more products or not. In fact some of the more ruthless multinationals (and their marketing people) I worked for, I would have quite enjoyed to have seen their sales take a downward plunge. I started thinking that when it came down to it all my really hard work and effort was being wasted. Some of the designs looked pretty good though!

**SAFIA** What is your vision for social and environmental justice?

**CHRIS** I think one of the biggest problems today is that multinationals are able to dodge laws too easily. They are effectively above the law. They need to be held to account a lot more than they are now, whether it is enforced by effective international law or from pressure from an educated public. I think transparency is very important. If people could see the difference that their choices made, their buying choices would be very different.

*"I found it very difficult to understand how such hardworking people could be so poor."*

Nobody wants to treat people unfairly, but the problem is that all these transactions are happening outside our view. The only way we can see or hear from the people that we effectively make transactions with every day of our lives is when the media shows us a story of injustice. If the public knew more they would change but the companies involved have an interest in clouding the issues. I have a lot of hope for the transparency that the internet can bring.

**SAFIA** Does it matter to you that People Tree can never pay you your market rate? We pay you in T-shirts and handmade notebooks and Fair Trade chocolate instead.

**CHRIS** No! I still love working for People Tree. It's very satisfying to work with something that is making a difference, also I have to say that the people I have met in People Tree are fantastic, as a freelance illustrator I have worked for literally hundreds of different companies and I can honestly say that I don't think that any of them have the same passion about what they do. It's been very life-affirming after working with marketing teams. Also the chocolate is very good.

**SAFIA** Where would you like to see your designs on People Tree handmade paper products sold?

**CHRIS** McDonald's.

**Chris Haughton**

Chris Haughton was born in Dublin in 1978. He illustrates regularly for The Guardian and often for The Times, and The Independent and many other publications. He was listed in Time magazine's DESIGN 100 last year for the work he has been doing for Fair Trade and People Tree. His website is at vegetablefriedrice.com

# Getting
## involved.

This might sound obvious, but the whole point of Fair Trade is that it's a sustainable business. So, if you are keen to support Fair Trade, buy Fair Trade products – next time you buy new clothes, look first to Fair Trade fashion! And why not introduce your friends to Fair Trade too.

Or go one step further – perhaps you want to become a Fair Trader selling Fair Trade products or run a Fair Trade event? Do you run a shop, and want to purchase some Fair Trade garments wholesale? Maybe you are looking for an internship or perhaps even a career with us?

You can find out about all these on our website **www.peopletree.co.uk,** and you can keep in regular touch by subscribing to our e-newsletters.

# Become a fair
## trader.

Promote Fair Trade and responsible shopping — a practical way to help alleviate poverty and promote development in communities in the developing world.

People Tree Fair Traders get discounts of up to 20%, special offers, free delivery on bulk orders and invites to People Tree events. Show our catalogue to your friends and colleagues and order together. Ask us for extra catalogues and distribute them to people at work. Use our fashion show kit to present a mini fashion show at local community events – or even hold your own.

You can do as little or as much as you like. Even just doing something for World Fair Trade Day in May or for Christmas shopping in November is a big help. By becoming a People Tree Fair Trader you'll help producers in the developing world get a better deal and play an important role in spreading the word in your local community about fairer fashion alternatives!

Fair finance
Fair trade

# Investing in people

**Fair trade reminds us that trade is about people and their futures.**

For over 30 years, Oikocredit has shared the values of fair trade and has also provided direct support for this sector. We offer credit where none is available from commercial banks. We work with producer cooperatives, small and medium-sized enterprises and microfinance institutions around the world.

Credit for development works. Started as a pioneer in the field of development financing in 1975, Oikocredit is today a leading expert in the field. Oikocredit is one of the few ethical investment funds which finances development projects that benefit disadvantaged and marginalized people in the South.

Oikocredit's loans are channeled through a unique network of 30 offices spread across Latin America, Asia, Africa and Central and Eastern Europe. These offices are managed by local professionals. Mid 2008, Oikocredit financed over 700 projects and had outstanding capital of some € 326 million.

**Responding to the need of credit for development.**

Oikocredit
*investing in people*

*www.oikocredit.org*

# Fair Trade groups say ...

"Today People Tree support has meant that we have doubled the number of people who are benefiting from Fair Trade to 543 people, as well as increasing their earnings by 50% in the last two years alone. This enabled widows and low-income men and women to educate their kids, put healthy food on the table for their families and save for the future."

—Prodip Gomes, deputy director, Folk Bangladesh

"People Tree changed our thinking and raised our expectations with their activity / action plan. Passing on the skills to run a business, make quality products, they gave us hope to develop our business. It also helped us to create a local market for our products. Our producers' incomes are increasing. For example some of our weavers have started their own hand loom businesses."

—Monjurul Haque, manager, Artisan Hut, Bangladesh

"People Tree is not just promoting Fair Trade products – it is promoting communities."

—Norma Velasquez, director of Minka Fair Trade

"People Tree has supported the development and growth of organic farming at Agrocel. Every year Agrocel is able to include more organic farmers in their group thanks to growing People Tree orders for organic cotton. People Tree also helps us with the improvement of our cotton."

— Hashmukh Patel, Agrocel Cooperative, India

"KTS mission is to provide free education to the needy children and to provide vocational training with job opportunities for underprivileged women, disabled people and widows. Every year we have around 60 knitwear graduates. People Tree UK orders have provided jobs for 452 women and profits cover the running costs of the school."

—Kiran Khadgi, Kumbeshwar Technical School (KTS), Nepal

"People Tree is committed to Fair Trade; therefore it is certainly much better than the mainstream buyers. It provides sustainable support, fair price, product development, environmental awareness and overall support for the development of grassroots artisans."

—Moon Sharma, Tara Projects, India

# Symbols of
# change ...

## IFAT – International Fair Trade Association

IFAT's mission is to improve the livelihoods and well being of disadvantaged producers by linking and promoting Fair Trade organisations, and speaking out for the greater justice in world trade. More than 265 members in 60 countries across the world have come together in solidarity and mutual co-operation to create an alternative and fairer way of doing business. People Tree joined IFAT in 1996.

## Fairtrade standards for cotton farmers

Almost all People Tree's organic cotton fibre is certified organic and Fairtrade. The FAIRTRADE Mark is a guarantee that small-scale cotton farmers in developing countries receive a fair and stable price. They also receive a premium payment for community development projects, such as promoting health awareness in schools.

## Organic standards in garment production

People Tree's organic cotton is not only grown to meet organic standards, the garments are also manufactured to meet organic standards. People Tree was the first company to be awarded the Soil Association mark for organic products made in the developing world. The Soil Association symbol guarantees products meet the Global Organic Textile standards (GOTS), ensuring environmentally friendly processes in tailoring, spinning, knitting fabric, transportation and storage.

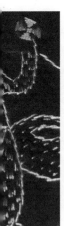

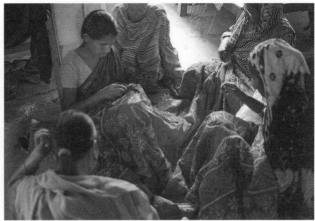

## Organic standards in cotton farming

Our cotton jersey is made with cotton to international organic standards by Control Union and Ecocert. This guarantees that cotton has been grown to strict organic standards. This protects that farmers' health, land and water from pollution, promoting sustainability. Organic farming also protects the farmer from the expense of chemical input, to achieve economic security, community development and genuine sustainability.

## Handknit

People Tree provides valuable employment for over 1,500 hand knitters throughout the world. Handknitting of clothing and accessories promotes livelihoods as well as creates jobs preparing wool, cotton, banana, silk and hemp fibres.

## Handwoven

One piece of clothing made with handwoven fabric employs 10 more people than a machine made piece. At the same time we are reviving an incredible but fast disappearing industry with no alternative employment for handweavers. Handweaving is the second largest industry in India after agriculture.

## Hand embroidered

People Tree works with hand embroiderers to provide design, technical and marketing assistance, helping to create livelihoods as well as helping keep alive traditional skills and make modern designs.

# FAQs

## Q. Who benefits from Fair Trade?

**A.** We all do. Most importantly, Fair Trade enables producers in the poorest communities of the world to work their way out of poverty, and look forward to a more positive future for themselves, their families and their communities. Fair Trade is not just about paying a fair price and meeting the legal standards on working conditions – it's a different way of doing business, a partnership that we can all benefit from. See www.peopletree.co.uk/socialreviewintroduction.php for more about how we all benefit from Fair Trade.

## Q. Is it possible to run a Fair Trade company on a large scale?

**A.** The fashion market is tough and Fair Trade fashion is even tougher. It takes a great deal of effort, commitment, skill and energy to build up the capacity of a small social enterprise in India or Bangladesh, so it can provide decent livelihoods for hundreds or even thousands of people. But some of the organisations we work with have grown to this size, and plenty of others are working towards this scale. For instance, KTS in Nepal, which makes hand-knitted garments and accessories for People Tree, supports over 2,000 people alongside its diverse social programmes. There are millions of people with traditional skills who could benefit, given the right technical assistance and a market that is receptive to Fair Trade fashion.

## Q. Are consumers becoming more ethically aware and thinking more about which clothes they buy? Why is this?

**A.** People are becoming increasingly aware of the environmental and social cost of fashion – and they know that their choices can make a difference. Fair Trade and ethical fashion is growing: there are already millions of cotton farmers and artisans and their families benefiting from fair trade, technical assistance and community development projects. Where five years ago there were hardly any, now every city in the UK has a boutique which only stocks ethical and fair trade clothing. People are starting to discern between only Fairtrade cotton fibre and fully fair trade manufacture. Consumers are also starting to ask for their Fairtrade cotton fibre to be organically certified too, creating

best practice in this area. That's why People Tree has not only pioneered the Fair Trade cotton and manufacture supply chain, but also campaigned to build awareness of the benefits of Fair Trade fashion, and works together with NGOs to campaign for change.

## Q. Where can I get more information on Fair Trade fashion?

**A.** To discover more about the principles and the diversity of organisations internationally, the best starting point is the International Fair Trade Association (IFAT), at www.ifat.org. For more facts and figures, the Fairtrade Foundation, www.fairtrade.co.uk and the Fairtrade Labelling Organisations International Annual reports at www.fairtrade.net/publications_media.html also have a fair amount of detail. For an insight into the social review system which underpins IFAT membership, see People Tree's Social Review on www.peopletree.co.uk/socialreviewintroduction.php. As for the practical details of running a Fair Trade organisation, my blog on www.peopletree.co.uk/safia will give you an insight into issues we run up against from day to day.

## Q. Where can I get more information about the issues, and about ethical fashion?

**A.** 'Fashioning an Ethical Industry' promotes awareness of social responsibility issues to fashion students and their tutors, and produces educational materials, courses and seminars. See fashioninganethicalindustry.org/home.

To find out more about abuses and root causes of poverty in the fashion industry, check out the Clean Clothes Campaign and its UK based platform, Labour behind the Label, www.labourbehindthelabel.org, War on Want campaigns www.waronwant.org, and Pesticide Action Network at www.pan-uk.org (follow the Quick Link to 'Wear Organic'). Ethical Fashion Forum at www.ethicalfashionforum.com has some information, as has the Ethical Trading Initiative (ETI) at www.ethicaltrade.org, a voluntary initiative by conventional businesses.

## Q. How do I start a Fair Trade business?

**A.** Starting a Fair Trade business is much the same as any business, but with added burdens. If you want to start a shop, the British Association of Fair Traders (www.bafts.org.uk) is a useful network and can put you in touch with Fair Trade producers. If you are interested in fashion design, Fashioning an Ethical industry and the ETI have some useful fact sheets.

## Q. Are Fair Trade products more expensive than other clothing?

**A.** People Tree aims to make Fair Trade fashion accessible to as wide an audience as possible, so we work hard to keep our prices down. There are significantly higher costs involved in producing Fair Trade clothing. The average Fair Trade and organic t-shirt of comparable quality is 50% more expensive than conventional, and a handwoven or handcrafted top would be three times more expensive than a machine-made one. In Fair Trade, 50% advances are given, up to 9 months before the product reaches you, and this adds to the cost. There are significant costs in the technical assistance we give producers in their villages.

We try to cover these extra costs as far as we can, and communicate the uniqueness of the product so that the customer appreciates the uniqueness of the product.

Producing clothing to Fair Trade standards throughout the supply chain is both challenging and expensive, which is probably why people Tree is the only company in the world doing 100% Fair Trade Fashion.

## Q. Does meeting environmental challenges have costs too?

**A.** All of our jersey cotton is made with certified organic cotton fibre, and we pay 30% more for this than the conventional cotton price. There are extra costs in making the textiles, and in purchasing dyes that conform to organic textile standards. We are also pioneers in this field, and it has take a lot of time and effort to develop and establish reliable sources for it. We are currently promoting the growing of organic cotton in Bangladesh, where there is none at the moment.

## Q. How trend-led is People Tree?

**A.** We aim to make stylish clothes that suit you and are versatile, so you want to wear them for longer. We lead the trend in many areas – in pioneering the use of organic cotton, sustainable textiles, handskills and Fair Trade fashion itself. (Our work is often covered in fashion industry trend books.) As far as following style trends, we have our ears close to the ground, but do our own thing most of the time. People Tree products are handmade, even the organic cotton has to be ordered a year or so before the products reach you – so we have to. We can't just produce something new because it's trendy and get it in a store in 6–8 weeks, which is how mass-produced fashion works.

## Q. Are there any design constraints working solely with ecologically sound fabrics and dyes?

**A.** People Tree uses only natural textiles, which limits the range of fabrics we can use. We cannot source the highest grades of organic cotton easily, which limits even the range of cotton fabrics we can work with. We don't use plastisol, which is used to print light colours on a dark background – so we only print dark designs on lighter backgrounds. Although the colour range of dyes produced to organic standards has widened, there are still limitations, particularly with blues and greens.

Our designers have to design clothes within these constraints, making best use of producers' traditional skills to maximise the benefit to producers.

# INVEST WITH **SHARED INTEREST** AND YOUR MONEY **SUPPORTS** **FAIR TRADE ENTERPRISES** IN THE WORLD'S POOREST COUNTRIES

**WE SEE A WORLD WHERE PEOPLE CAN TRADE AS EQUALS**

The jewellery shown was created by Umtha (meaning 'Ray of Light'), a fair trade business in Cape Town, South Africa. Umtha first started in a converted garage in 1992, but thanks to support from Shared Interest, they have grown the business, taken on new employees and developed a wider range of products which are successfully sold through the fair trade network. The business offers its employees the stability to grow and develop as individuals, providing support for their families and helping break the cycle of poverty in the next generation.

Images courtesy of Umtha

Become a member of Shared Interest and you can help support other businesses like Umtha throughout the developing world. You can join a growing number of people who see support for fair trade as a key means of addressing global poverty. We want members who share our vision of a world where communities can trade as equals and where justice, not profit, is the bottom line.

It's easy to become a member, and for as little as £100 you can open an account. For more information call us on (0)191 233 9100 quoting PT1 or visit our website at www.shared-interest.com

# SHAREDINTEREST

## INVESTING IN A FAIRER WORLD

# FAIR TRADE
# AT THE G8

*Hokkaido Japan, 7th – 9th July 2008*
In the run-up to the G8 summit, People Tree and the Fair Trade
movement called on the G8 leaders to make Fair Trade a priority.

## G8 leadership is needed in three key areas:

### 1. Recognise Fair Trade as a model of environmental and social justice

The G8 has largely ignored the
environmental initiatives and innovations used by the Fair
Trade and social enterprise movements. Because Fair Trade
works in long term partnership, producers are able to 'invest' in
environmental protection and carbon neutral production. For
example, Fair Trade organic cotton producers in Gujarat save
1.5 tonnes of $CO_2$ per acre per year sequestered in the soil (not
to mention saving $CO_2$ generated in making oil-based pesticides).
One hand weaver in Bangladesh saves 1 tonne of $CO_2$ per year.
Carbon credit programmes should be funded to build the capacity
of small-scale producers; after all, it is the poor in the developing
world that have the lightest environmental footprint.

when there is a substantial risk of missing Millennium
Development Goal targets if economic growth is not achieved
in developing countries.

### 2. Change trade rules to focus on the poor

G8 members' trade policy remains
unconnected to the real circumstances of poor producers in
developing countries. Their past approach to trade policy has
favoured liberalisation and free trade as a response to poverty. In
our experience this theory frequently does not work in practice
and it is often the poorest people who suffer most as a result.
Developing countries should have the right to nurture and protect
vulnerable and emerging sectors of their economies from free and
unfettered trade until they are able to compete regionally and
internationally. No country, G8 members included, has developed
without protection. This pragmatic – rather than theoretical –
approach should be the bedrock of G8 trade policy, especially

### 3. Make businesses act more responsibly

Most companies still do not take proper
account of their social and environmental impact. The Fair Trade
movement has developed standards and assessment processes
that show best practice in this area. The G8 should develop an
ambitious strategy for the private sector, with key performance
indicators (economic, social and environmental) which focus on
the impact that trade has on poverty. Robust regulation is needed
to correct the imbalance of power between multinational retailers
and their suppliers. This would set out companies' responsibilities
for their social and environmental impacts and give workers,
farmers or suppliers harmed by a company's activities the chance
to seek redress.

# Design and technical

## assistance

### Practical help on hand

By giving design and technical assistance, Fair Trade reaches the people that other trade does not. People Tree has one of the biggest design and technical assistance teams in the Fair Trade movement. Worldwide, 20 people work on product quality, technical and capacity-building support and the design renewal that fashion demands. Some see working with People Tree as a 'quality mark' in itself. We spend months every year working with producers in their villages, and once back home, we continue our support via email and phone. We help to solve problems including getting good quality materials and accessories, and strengthening environmental production processes. Right from the top of the organisation, we are involved in helping producer groups strengthen their organisations, financing and helping them identify and overcome barriers to scaling up their work. This isn't just buying from a Fair Trade group, this is building a Fair Trade and environmentally friendly supply chain from scratch.

### Design starts with traditional and hand skills

Unlike a conventional fashion company, People Tree doesn't start with concepts and designs alone – we start with the traditional hand skills and the unique craftsmanship of each group. Products are designed to maximise the number of people that earn a living through making the product. A mass produced top may take only 12 minutes to make, but a handwoven, hand embellished top can provide employment for between one to three days. People Tree designers thrive on the creative challenge of working with traditional skills, hand production methods, and natural materials; they work closely with the craftspeople to innovate and use these skills in a contemporary way – exciting things can be achieved by working closely together. We start planning our designs six to nine months before the majority of the fashion industry, to allow enough time for hand production. So, being a designer at People Tree is the ultimate creative challenge.

Patterning, tailoring and quality workshops are run regularly in the field. A market exposure programme enables Fair Trade partners to study the market where their products sell, work with designers, and meet their customers. People Tree also gets involved in supporting groups with cost accounting, production management, business planning, and developing their capacity to achieve certification for organic, environmental and Fair Trade standards.

## Helping Fair Trade groups to go green

People Tree sets the pace in environmental practice too, having developed the first Fair Trade and organic supply chain to deliver 100% Fairly Traded clothing to the market. In 1996 we launched the EcoTextile project to help Fair Trade producers convert to azo-free dyes – many azo dyes are carcinogenic for the wearer, and once in the waterways following production, affect the health of local people too. We ruled out the use of chlorine bleach – to avoid dioxins, some of the most harmful toxins known to man. In 2006 we launched the first Soil Association organic certified garment from the developing world to meet GOTS (Global Organic Textile Standards), together with Assisi Garments. In 2007 we launched the first organic cotton project in Bangladesh with Waste Concern and local Fair Trade partners. People Tree uses natural materials in all clothing and natural biodegradable buttons and accessories where possible. We also maximise what we can import by sea freight, currently more than 95%. That's on top of the 6–8 months production time – the antithesis of fast fashion, this is slow fashion!

# People Tree store

## in Tokyo

People Tree opened its first stand-alone store in Tokyo in 1998 and the Fair Trade Fashion franchise store in 2006 in Aoyama, the fashion centre of Tokyo. We look forward to bringing our first store to London in 2009.

# Stockists

**UK
STOCKISTS**

AMERICAN PIE
LONDON, Kingston
ARKADASH
MANCHESTER, Chorlton
B FAIR
NORFOLK, Little Walsingham
BETTY AND BABS
CUMBRIA, Kendal
CARLISLE WORLD SHOP
CUMBRIA, Carlisle
COVET
SUSSEX, Brighton
EQUA
LONDON, Islington
EXCLUSIVE ROOTS
WARWICKSHIRE, Warwick
FAIR DOS
WALES, Cardiff
FAIR TRADE INSPIRES
NORTHERN IRELAND, Belfast
FAIRTRADE AT ST MICHAELS
OXFORDSHIRE, Oxford
FAMILY TREE
LONDON, Exmouth Market
FINESSE LIFESTYLE
LONDON, Tower Hamlets
FIRST LIGHT
WALES, Abersoch
FOAM FASHION
BERKSHIRE, Henley on Thames
FREE RANGE
OXFORDSHIRE, Thame
FYNE LIVING
SCOTLAND, Argyll
GREEN DRAWERS
DORSET, Beaminster
GREEN SQUIRREL
SCOTLAND, Perth

GREENWAY STORES
BEDFORDSHIRE,
Leighton Buzzard
HARVEST MOON
HEREDFORDSHIRE, Hitchin
JUSTICE UK
DERBYSHIRE, Buxton
KINGDOM KRAFTS
GWYNEDD, Llandudno
KIS EMPORIUM
DORSET, Shaftesbury
KOLKATA
SUSSEX, Brighton
(Preston Park)
LAND OF GREEN GINGER
ISLE OF GUERNSEY,
St Peter Port
MARCOS AND TRUMP
LONDON, Columbia Road
MOO BOUTIQUE
CHESHIRE, Stockport
ONE BTQ
YORKSHIRE, York
ONE WORLD SHOP
SCOTLAND, Edinburgh
ONE WORLD SHOP
SCOTLAND, Glasgow
ORCHID
DORSET, Dorchester
OXFAM BTQ
BUCKINGHAMSHIRE,
Gerrards Cross
OXFAM BTQ
LONDON, Chiswick
OXFAM BTQ
LONDON, Kings Road
OXFAM BTQ
LONDON, Westbourne Grove

OXFAM BTQ
SCOTLAND, Edinburgh,
Morningside
OXFAM BTQ
WILTSHIRE, Salisbury
OXFAM IRELAND
Selected stores
PURITY
SURREY, Farnham
QUINTESSENTIALLY
WILKSHIRE, Lacock
REJUVENATE
SOMERSET, Clevedon
ROCOCO BOUTIQUE
LONDON, Muswell Hill
SECRET WARDROBE
DORSET, Sidmouth
SHAKTI MAN
ISLE OF MAN, Ramsey
SHOON
LONDON, Marylebone
SHOON
SOMERSET, Bath
SPIRALS
LANCASHIRE, Hebden Bridge
STELLA WOMENSWEAR
LONDON, Camden
STOKED
LANCASHIRE, Liverpool
TAURUS CRAFT
GLOUCESTERSHIRE, Lydney
TERRA PLANA
LONDON, Bermondsey Street
TERRA PLANA
LONDON, Neal's Street
THE BETTER FOOD CO
SOMERSET, Bristol
(St Werburgh)

THE CONKER SHOE CO
DEVON, Totnes
THE GREEN HOUSE
WILTSHIRE, Salisbury
THE GREEN SHOP
NORTHUMBERLAND,
Berwick uon Tweed
TIGER LILY
SHROPSHIRE, Ludlow
TIMBER
HAMPSHIRE, Ringwood
TOPSHOP CONCESSION
LONDON, Oxford Street
and selected stores
TRENABIES
ORKNEY ISLAND, Kirkwall
UNEEKA
CORNWALL, Truro
WARDROBE
SUFFOLK, Stowmarket
WICKLE
SUSSEX, Lewes

## UK
## WEBSITE

ADILI.com
ASOS.com
ECOCHICFAIRTRADE.co.uk
ETHICALSUPERSTORE.com
FAIRTRADEBOUTIQUE.co.uk
SUST:SOUTHIC.com
THENATURALSTORE.co.uk
OXFAM.org.uk
TOPSHOP.com
NEWINTERNATIONALIST.org.uk

## UK
## MAIL ORDER

NEW INTERNATIONALIST

## IRISH
## STOCKIST

MIRA MIRA

## IRISH
## WEBSITE

BELLEETIK.com

## INTERNATIONAL
## STOCKISTS

VZW SJAMMA
BELGIUM, Gent
ECO MAMMA SRO
CZECH REP, Praha
BAZAREN
DENMARK, Århus
ECO EGO
DENMARK, Copenhagen
SUB:STANZ
DENMARK, Copenhagen
TERRA PURA
FRANCE, Clermont-Ferrand
FAIRTRAGEN
GERMANY, Bremen
SUBURBIA
GERMANY, Dusseldorf
IKI M
GERMANY, Munich
VALEVIDA
GERMANY, Peiting
GAIA SKREATION
GREECE, Crete
PARTICELLE COMPLIMENTARI
ITALY, Milan
SMARAGDO MIESTAS
LITHUANIA
BRENNELS
NETHERLANDS, Arnhem
WERELDMODEWINKEL SARI
NETHERLANDS, Dalfsen
SARI LOCHEM
NETHERLANDS, Lochem
SANSELIV
NORWAY, Bergen
FRIENDS FAIRTRADE
NORWAY, Oslo
FAIRPLAY
NORWAY, Stavanger

ECOLOGIQUE
ROUMANIA, Bucharest
JANINA – UK D.O.0
SLOVENIA, Ljubljana
OLOKUTI
SPAIN, Barcelona
PERSPECTIVE
SPAIN, Mallorca
BERTHAS EKO AB
SWEDEN, Gothenburg
THE FAIR TRADE SHOP
SWEDEN, Stockholm
VARLDSBUTIKEN SOLEN
SWEDEN, Alingsas
UMA BAZAAR
SWEDEN, Malmö
AWEARNESS
SWEDEN, Nykoping
VÄRLDSBUTIKEN UMEÅ
SWEDEN, Umeå
VÄRLDSBUTIKEN GLOBA
SWEDEN, Uppsala
VÄRLDSBUTIKEN HELSI
SWEDEN, Helsingborg
VÄRLDSBUTIKEN KUNGÄ
SWEDEN, Kungälv
VÄRLDSBUTIKEN KLOTET
SWEDEN, Lund

## INTERNATIONAL
## WEBSITE

COMPTOIR ETHIQUE.com
KARMA.com
MODETIC.com
EKO ALTERNATIWA.com

## PEOPLE TREE
## STORES JAPAN

People Tree Jiyugaoka
3-7-2 Jiyugaoka,
Meguro-ku, Tokyo
phone 03 5701 3361

People Tree Omotesando
5-12-10 Jingumae,
Shibuya-ku, Tokyo
phone 03 5469 6333

For People Tree stockists
in Japan see:
http://www.peopletree.co.jp/
shop_oroshi/index.html

## People Tree
www.peopletree.co.uk

FAIR PLAY

People Tree

Streets ahead

METROSTYLE

People Tree
the Fair Trade Fashion pioneer

Foundation Addict

TRIBAL

# *Thank you …*

## Thank you to all these people who helped People Tree to tell our tale …

Andreas Pohancenik of Zwei Ltd, Nick Robertson, Emma Mclaughlin, Jo Hunt, Bora and Fella Aksu, Richard Nicoll, Thakoon, Sam Ubhi, Chris Haughton, Anne Watanabe, Helena Christensen, Rama Photography, Miki Alcalde, Annoushka Giltsoff, Boo Kyoung Lee, Tetsuhara Kubota, Leeyong, Vogue Nippon, Louise Thestrup, Joey Coombs, Mura Collective, Agrocel, Asos.com, Oikocredit, Shared Interest, Tatami Japan, Liz Hitchcock, Dominic Wells, Imogen Stevens, Rowena Young, Jane Shepherdson, Phil King, Tim Morgan, Roger Perowne, Alex Nicholls, Kees van den Burg, Polly Hope, and Ranjith Henry, who sowed the seed of this idea in my mind, and to the artisans and Fair Trade groups who helped contribute to this book …

## … and everyone who is helping to change lives by choosing Fair Trade.

---

**IMPRINT**

**Editorial Support**
James Minney, Liz Hitchcock, Dominic Wells, Antony Waller, Hannah Davey, Deborah Isaacs

**Art Direction and Layout**
Zwei Ltd

**Book Photography**
Safia Minney, Miki Alcalde

**Fashion Photography**
Rama Photography, Annoushka Giltsoff, Boo Kyoung Lee, Richard Burns, Helena Christensen, Tetsuhara Kubota

**Front Cover**
Rama Photography
Model: Sosheba Griffiths

**Illustrations**
Chris Haughton

**Production**
Sarah Tolley, Lucy Hall, Kitty Pennybacker,

**Repro**
F1 Colour

**Printing**

CAMBRIAN
**CP**
PRINTERS

**Paper**

H Robert Horne Group

Printed on revive 50:50 Offset, a recycled paper containing 50% recovered waste and 50% Forest Stewardship Council (FSC) certified pulp and elemental chlorine free, supplied exclusively by the Robert Horne Group. Printed by Cambrian Printers using vegetable based inks. Both Cambrian Printers and Robert Horne are ISO 14001:2004 accredited and hold FSC Chain of Custody.